TRIUMPH

TRIUMPH

HUGO WILSON

DK

DORLING KINDERSLEY
DK PUBLISHING, INC.

A DK PUBLISHING BOOK

PROJECT EDITOR PHIL HUNT
ART EDITOR MARK JOHNSON DAVIES

SENIOR EDITOR LOUISE CANDLISH
SENIOR ART EDITOR HEATHER McCARRY
MANAGING EDITOR ANNA KRUGER
DEPUTY ART DIRECTOR TINA VAUGHAN
US EDITOR RAY ROGERS
PRODUCTION CONTROLLER ALISON JONES

First American edition, 1998

2 4 6 8 10 9 7 5 3 1

Published in the United States by DK Publishing, Inc.,
95 Madison Avenue, New York, New York 10016

Visit us on the World Wide Web at http://www.dk.com

Library of Congress Cataloging-in-Publication Data

Wilson, Hugo
    Triumph / by Hugo Wilson. -- 1st American ed.
        p.   cm. -- (Classic motorcycles)
    ISBN 0-7894-3507-1
    1. Triumph motorcycle--History.   I. Title II. Series.
TL448.T7W547   1998
629.227'5--dc21

98-17160
CIP

Reproduced by Colourscan, Singapore
Printed in Hong Kong

CONTENTS

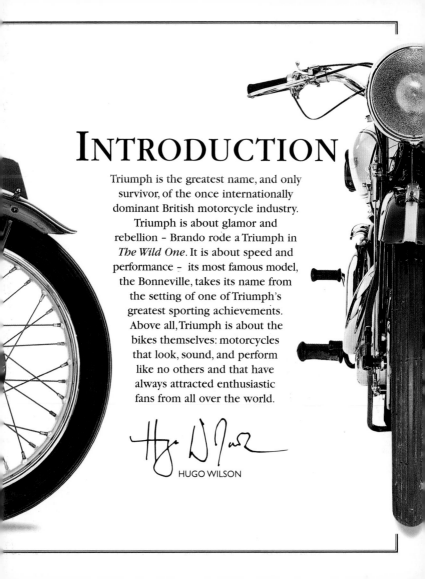

INTRODUCTION

Triumph is the greatest name, and only
survivor, of the once internationally
dominant British motorcycle industry.
Triumph is about glamor and
rebellion – Brando rode a Triumph in
The Wild One. It is about speed and
performance – its most famous model,
the Bonneville, takes its name from
the setting of one of Triumph's
greatest sporting achievements.
Above all, Triumph is about the
bikes themselves: motorcycles
that look, sound, and perform
like no others and that have
always attracted enthusiastic
fans from all over the world.

HUGO WILSON

TRIUMPH TIMELINE

Britain's OLDEST AND ONLY SURVIVING manufacturer of motorcycles was originally a bicycle maker. The company has progressed dramatically from producing bicycles with an engine to manufacturing astonishingly high-performance machines. The only similarity between the original bike and the superbikes of today is the name and the number of wheels.

MINERVA

THE EARLY DAYS

Triumph's early bicycle origins are obvious in this early Minerva model, which is no more than a bicycle with an engine. As long as engines weren't powerful enough to propel bicycles without the aid of pedals, the machine would continue to look like a bicycle.

• 1910s	• 1920s	• 1930s	• 1940s	• 1950s

R TYPE FAST ROADSTER

THE 1930s

Mechanically, little had changed since the 1920s, but the design had sleeker lines. Drum brakes were fitted and chrome added to improve the look of the machine.

THE 1920s

The design had now moved on so that the engine was placed in the frame between the downtubes and the top frame-rail bent to allow a lower seating position. The effect was a lower, longer bike than before.

TIGER 80

QUINTESSENTIAL TRIUMPH

For nearly 50 years, the Triumph name was associated with parallel twins and for many fans Triumph is still the classic British motorcycle. In 1937, its 500cc machine was considered an innovative and sporting motorcycle, and the same forward-thinking design was evident in this 1959 T120 Bonneville.

Parallel twin first introduced in 1937

T120 BONNEVILLE

• 1960s	• 1970s	• 1980s	• 1990s

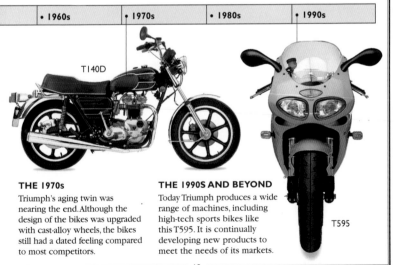

T140D

T595

THE 1970s

Triumph's aging twin was nearing the end. Although the design of the bikes was upgraded with cast-alloy wheels, the bikes still had a dated feeling compared to most competitors.

THE 1990S AND BEYOND

Today Triumph produces a wide range of machines, including high-tech sports bikes like this T595. It is continually developing new products to meet the needs of its markets.

1902 MINERVA

• TRIUMPH ENTERS THE WORLD OF MOTORCYCLES •

AS AN ESTABLISHED BICYCLE MAKER, Triumph followed the recognized
method of making a motorcycle at the turn of the 20th century – bolting
an engine, fuel tank, and drive belt to a modified bicycle. This 1902
machine is fitted with a Belgian Minerva engine. While
the mechanically operated inlet and exhaust
valves and the spray carburetor make it more
sophisticated than many contemporaries,
it would have been unreliable,
uncomfortable, and awkward to ride.

Carburetor and
ignition controls

License plate

Bicycle light

Bicycle-type
stirrup brake on
front wheel

TRIUMPH

Braced
front fork

Engine
mounting clamp

MINER

SIDE VIEW

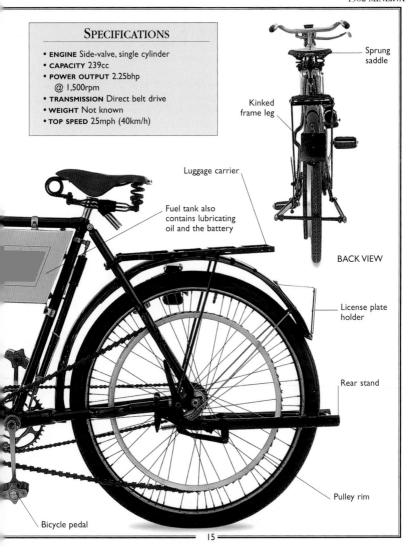

SPECIFICATIONS

- **ENGINE** Side-valve, single cylinder
- **CAPACITY** 239cc
- **POWER OUTPUT** 2.25bhp @ 1,500rpm
- **TRANSMISSION** Direct belt drive
- **WEIGHT** Not known
- **TOP SPEED** 25mph (40km/h)

Sprung saddle

Kinked frame leg

BACK VIEW

Luggage carrier

Fuel tank also contains lubricating oil and the battery

License plate holder

Rear stand

Pulley rim

Bicycle pedal

1910 HUB CLUTCH

• A SMOOTHER RIDE WITH IMPROVED RELIABILITY •

TRIUMPH STARTED MAKING ITS OWN single-cylinder side-valve engines in 1905 and fitted them into strengthened frames in front of the pedals. A sprung fork smoothed the ride slightly, and magneto ignition meant that there were fewer roadside breakdowns. This 1910 model has another innovation: the "Patent Free Engine Hub Clutch" allowed the engine to be kept running while the bike was stationary. It also meant that a gearbox and kick-start could be fitted, but these additions came later. The clutch was operated by a foot pedal and was fitted into the rear hub between the drive pulley and the wheel.

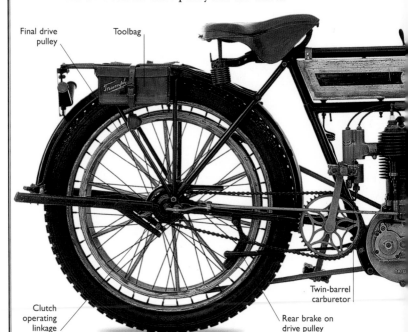

Final drive pulley

Toolbag

Clutch operating linkage

Twin-barrel carburetor

Rear brake on drive pulley

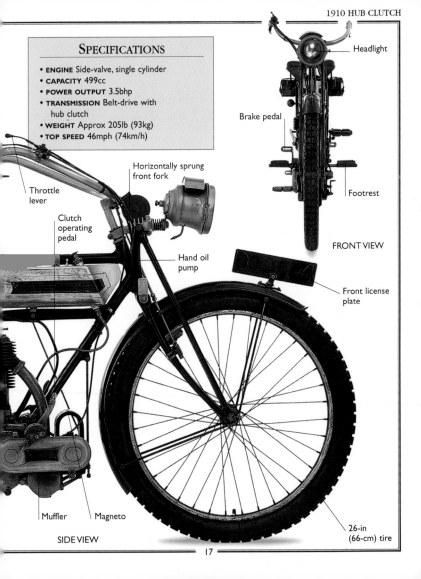

Headlight

Brake pedal

Footrest

FRONT VIEW

SPECIFICATIONS

- **ENGINE** Side-valve, single cylinder
- **CAPACITY** 499cc
- **POWER OUTPUT** 3.5bhp
- **TRANSMISSION** Belt-drive with hub clutch
- **WEIGHT** Approx 205lb (93kg)
- **TOP SPEED** 46mph (74km/h)

Horizontally sprung front fork

Throttle lever

Clutch operating pedal

Hand oil pump

Front license plate

Muffler

Magneto

SIDE VIEW

26-in (66-cm) tire

1920 KNIRPS
• A GERMAN VERSION OF A POPULAR MODEL •

TRIUMPH'S GERMAN BOSSES SET UP an offshoot of the Coventry-based company in their home town of Nürnberg in 1903, and in 1920 they produced the first Knirps ("Nipper"). The bike was based on the popular "Junior" Triumph that had been built in Coventry since 1913. It was Triumph's first two-stroke and was its base model for many years. The German version had a slightly increased capacity, and though a two-speed countershaft gearbox was fitted, there was no clutch or kick-start.

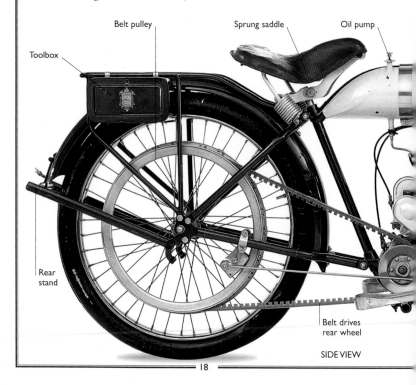

Belt pulley

Sprung saddle

Oil pump

Toolbox

Rear stand

Belt drives rear wheel

SIDE VIEW

SPECIFICATIONS

- **ENGINE** Two-stroke, single cylinder
- **CAPACITY** 276cc
- **POWER OUTPUT** 3bhp
- **TRANSMISSION** Two-speed, belt drive
- **WEIGHT** 130lb (59kg)
- **TOP SPEED** 40mph (64km/h)

TRIUMPH POSTER
The original British Triumph factory was in Coventry. After it was destroyed by German bombs in World War II, a new factory was built on a site outside the city at Meriden.

Gear change is controlled from handlebars

Gas tank

Sprung fork

Valanced mudguard

TRIUMPH

Rear brake pedal

1923 TYPE R FAST ROADSTER

• FOUR-VALVE TECHNOLOGY FOR THE 1920s •

THERE IS NEVER ANYTHING NEW in motorcycling. Enthusiasts got excited about four-valve cylinders in the 1960s and '70s, but pioneer manufacturers had known about the theoretical benefits nearly half a century earlier. Triumph's four-valver was designed by engineering consultant Harry Ricardo and was based on the conventional two-valve Model H. Introduced for the 1921 TT races, the machine remained in the catalog until 1927. However, Triumph concentrated its efforts on the two-valve design from 1924, and it wasn't until the four-valve head was used on short-stroke engines that the real benefits were exploited.

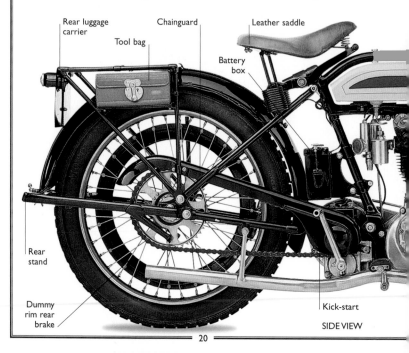

Rear luggage carrier

Tool bag

Chainguard

Leather saddle

Battery box

Rear stand

Dummy rim rear brake

Kick-start

SIDE VIEW

HARRY RICARDO

Ricardo realized that more valves in an engine meant improved fuel flow due to the greater valve area. Small, lighter valves reduce a unit's reciprocating mass and allow higher revs.

SPECIFICATIONS

- **ENGINE** Overhead-valve, single cylinder
- **CAPACITY** 499cc
- **POWER OUTPUT** 20bhp
- **TRANSMISSION** Three-speed
- **WEIGHT** 240lb (109kg)
- **TOP SPEED** 75mph (121km/h)

Hand oil pump

Gear change lever

Inverted control lever

Stirrup front brake

License plate

Magneto

Timing-gear case

Druid pattern girder fork

1934 6/1

• INNOVATION IN THE FORM OF A PARALLEL TWIN-CYLINDER •

W HILE MANY MANUFACTURERS BEGAN building V-twins, Triumph stuck to its single-cylinder engines until 1933, when it unveiled a novel parallel twin-cylinder machine. The 649cc 6/1 model was developed by Triumph's design chief, Valentine Page, and was intended mainly for sidecar use. The innovative design had helical gear drive to the gearbox, which was bolted to the back of the engine. The camshaft was located behind the base of the cylinders and operated the valves via pushrods running in tunnels in the cylinder barrels. Although the parallel twin was to become a firm favorite with British manufacturers, the 6/1 was discontinued in 1936.

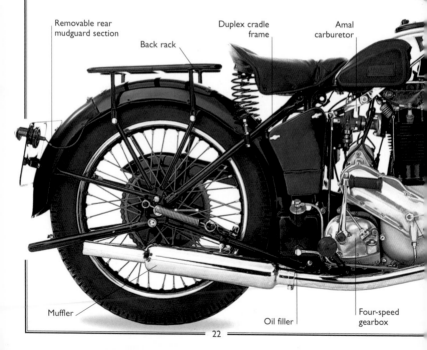

Removable rear
mudguard section

Back rack

Duplex cradle
frame

Amal
carburetor

Muffler

Oil filler

Four-speed
gearbox

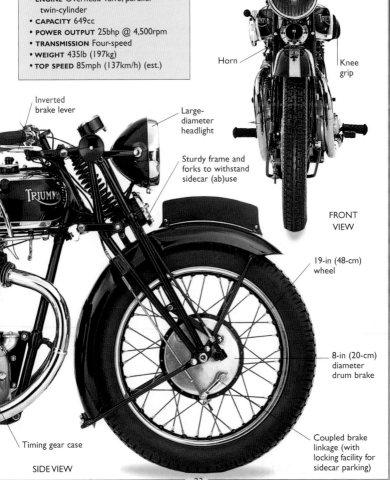

SPECIFICATIONS

- **ENGINE** Overhead-valve, parallel twin-cylinder
- **CAPACITY** 649cc
- **POWER OUTPUT** 25bhp @ 4,500rpm
- **TRANSMISSION** Four-speed
- **WEIGHT** 435lb (197kg)
- **TOP SPEED** 85mph (137km/h) (est.)

Horn

Knee grip

Inverted brake lever

Large-diameter headlight

Sturdy frame and forks to withstand sidecar (ab)use

FRONT VIEW

19-in (48-cm) wheel

8-in (20-cm) diameter drum brake

TRIUMPH

Timing gear case

SIDE VIEW

Coupled brake linkage (with locking facility for sidecar parking)

1937 TIGER 80
• AN OLD RANGE IS SUCCESSFULLY TRANSFORMED •

TRIUMPH WAS TAKEN OVER IN 1936, and one of the first things the new owners did was install Edward Turner (see p. 27) as design chief. His main priority was to revamp the capable but staid 250cc, 350cc, and 500cc overhead-valve singles. Chrome, polished alloy, and new paintwork improved the looks, and revised engines improved the performance. The bikes were relaunched as the Tiger 70, Tiger 80, and Tiger 90 – the numbers after the name were an optimistic indication of the speed of each model in miles per hour. The success of these new bikes helped ensure the survival of the Triumph marque.

Single exhaust port – previous model had two

Toolbox

2¾ x 3½in (70 x 89mm) engine has 7.5:1 compression ratio

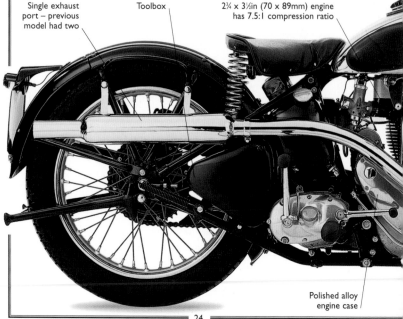

Polished alloy engine case

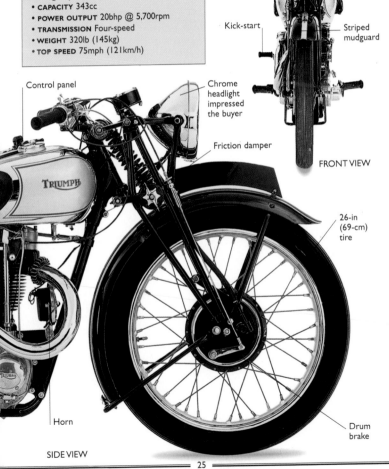

SPECIFICATIONS

- **ENGINE** Overhead-valve, single cylinder
- **CAPACITY** 343cc
- **POWER OUTPUT** 20bhp @ 5,700rpm
- **TRANSMISSION** Four-speed
- **WEIGHT** 320lb (145kg)
- **TOP SPEED** 75mph (121km/h)

Kick-start

Striped mudguard

FRONT VIEW

Control panel

Chrome headlight impressed the buyer

Friction damper

Triumph

26-in (69-cm) tire

Horn

Drum brake

SIDE VIEW

1939 SPEED TWIN

• TRIUMPH RAISES THE STANDARD TO A NEW LEVEL •

INTRODUCED IN 1937, THIS WAS THE MOST influential British bike ever made. The parallel twin-cylinder engine had a two-bearing crankshaft with a central flywheel and also had two camshafts (behind and in front of the cylinders) and enclosed valvegear. The new engine was mounted in the chassis of the Tiger 90. It offered a new level of power, performance, looks, and sophistication to motorbike buyers and was a template that other British manufacturers soon attempted to copy. The outbreak of war in 1939 delayed the arrival of a swarm of copycat parallel twins from other British factories. When they finally arrived, the Triumph outlived them all.

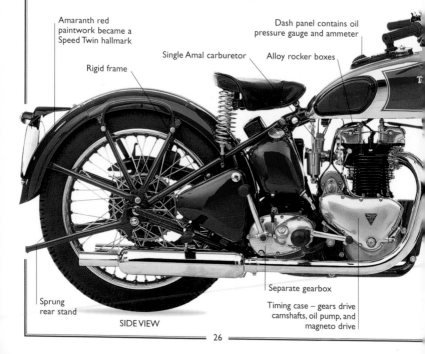

Amaranth red paintwork became a Speed Twin hallmark

Dash panel contains oil pressure gauge and ammeter

Single Amal carburetor

Alloy rocker boxes

Rigid frame

Separate gearbox

Sprung rear stand

Timing case – gears drive camshafts, oil pump, and magneto drive

SIDE VIEW

EDWARD TURNER

Turner was one of the most influential motorcycle designers of his era. Having worked at Ariel for a number of years, he moved to Triumph in 1936 and pioneered the use of chrome and color schemes on the company's Tiger range.

SPECIFICATIONS

- **ENGINE** Overhead-valve, parallel twin
- **CAPACITY** 498cc
- **POWER OUTPUT** 27bhp @ 6,300rpm
- **TRANSMISSION** Four-speed
- **WEIGHT** 378lb (171kg)
- **TOP SPEED** 93mph (150km/h)

License plate

8-in (20-cm) headlight

Kick-start

Footrest

Chrome exhaust

7-in (18-cm) drum brake

Speedometer drive cable

FRONT VIEW

1956 RECORD BREAKER

• TRIUMPH'S BONNEVILLE NAME IS ESTABLISHED •

TRIUMPHS SOLD IN LARGE NUMBERS in postwar America and soon became popular with racers and tuners. This cigar-shaped projectile played an essential part in establishing the Triumph legend. It was built by a team from Texas to beat the world land-speed record for motorcycles. The frame is a multitubular structure, and the tuned 649cc Thunderbird engine runs on alcohol. At the Bonneville Salt Flats in 1956, Johnny Allen sped to a new world-record speed of 214mph (345km/h). Even though the FIM (Federation of International Motorcyclists) refused to recognize the new record, the achievement gave Triumph its most famous model name – "Bonneville".

JOINT PROJECT

Although the Record Breaker used a Triumph engine, it was modified and fitted into a special frame by Jack Wilson and J.H. Mangham in Dallas, Texas. It underlined Triumph's popularity in America at that time.

Rider's cockpit is in front of the engine

Aerodynamic shell

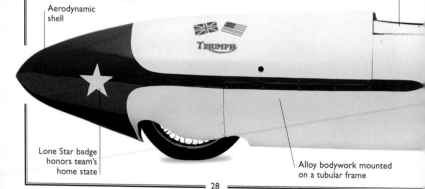

Lone Star badge honors team's home state

Alloy bodywork mounted on a tubular frame

GOOD PUBLICITY

Although the FIM didn't acknowledge the record, Triumph exploited the publicity value of the achievement with an advertising campaign. Over the next few years, Triumph-powered record-breakers continued to increase in speed.

SPECIFICATIONS

- **ENGINE** Modified Triumph Thunderbird air-cooled, overhead-valve twin
- **CAPACITY** 649cc
- **POWER OUTPUT** 65bhp (est.)
- **TRANSMISSION** Four-speed, chain drive
- **WEIGHT** Not disclosed
- **TOP SPEED** 214mph (345km/h)

FAST AND FLAT

The Bonneville Salt Flats are ideal for setting speed records. The huge expanse of flat salt means that bikes can build up speed before they pass through the timing lights at the beginning of their run and still have room to slow down.

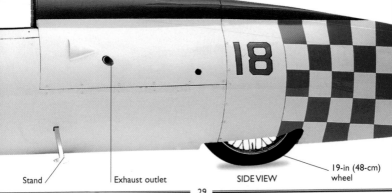

Stand

Exhaust outlet

SIDE VIEW

19-in (48-cm) wheel

1958 3TA

• TRIUMPH'S FIRST UNIT-CONSTRUCTION TWIN •

Triumph's new 3TA model was introduced in 1957. The new 350cc engine featured unitary construction of the engine and gearbox, which reduced costs and maintenance, and this feature was soon adopted for the bigger twins. An alternator was mounted on the left end of the crank, and ignition was by distributor. The 3TA also used the distinctive "bathtub" rear bodywork that was soon adopted across the range. The 350 was also named the Twenty One to reflect its capacity in US terminology – 21 cubic inches. A 490cc version was introduced in 1959.

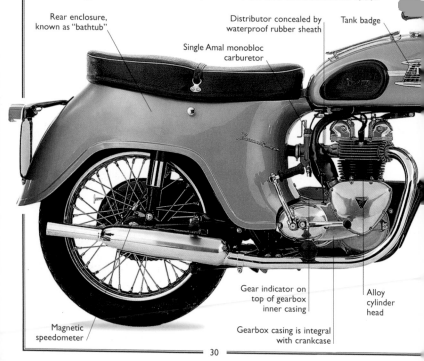

Rear enclosure, known as "bathtub"

Distributor concealed by waterproof rubber sheath

Tank badge

Single Amal monobloc carburetor

Gear indicator on top of gearbox inner casing

Alloy cylinder head

Gearbox casing is integral with crankcase

Magnetic speedometer

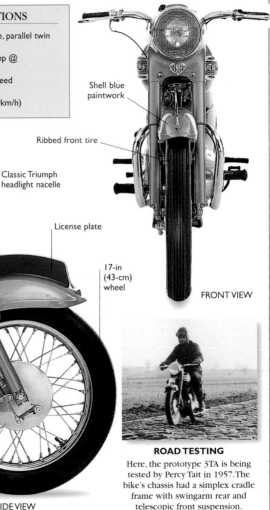

SPECIFICATIONS

- **ENGINE** Overhead-valve, parallel twin
- **CAPACITY** 349cc
- **POWER OUTPUT** 18.5bhp @ 6,500rpm
- **TRANSMISSION** Four-speed
- **WEIGHT** 349lb (158kg)
- **TOP SPEED** 80mph (129km/h)

Shell blue paintwork

Speedometer

Ribbed front tire

Classic Triumph headlight nacelle

License plate

17-in (43-cm) wheel

FRONT VIEW

7-in (18-cm) full-width front drum brake

SIDE VIEW

ROAD TESTING

Here, the prototype 3TA is being tested by Percy Tait in 1957. The bike's chassis had a simplex cradle frame with swingarm rear and telescopic front suspension.

1959 T20 Tiger Cub

• A BABY TRIUMPH WITH A BIG HEART •

In the years after World War II, Triumph was famous for its parallel twins, but the company also made smaller machines and scooters. Based on the earlier 149cc Terrier, the 199cc Tiger Cub was introduced in 1954 and remained in the range until 1968. The all-alloy engine had an inclined cylinder, and the four-speed gearbox was built in unit with the engine. Its light weight gave it good performance and easy handling. The Cub was a popular machine with learners and commuters, and trial versions were also successful.

Gear indicator

Telescopic fork

Braced front fork

Loop frame

Unit-construction engine with inclined cylinder

Lightweight drum brake

SIDE VIEW

go modern go TRIUMPH

SALES BROCHURE

Triumph emphasized advanced design and tchnology in its sales literature, but in reality the bikes were outdated when launched.

SPECIFICATIONS

- **ENGINE** Overhead-valve, single cylinder
- **CAPACITY** 199cc
- **POWER OUTPUT** 10bhp @ 6,000rpm
- **TRANSMISSION** Four-speed
- **WEIGHT** 240lb (109kg)
- **TOP SPEED** 72mph (116km/h)

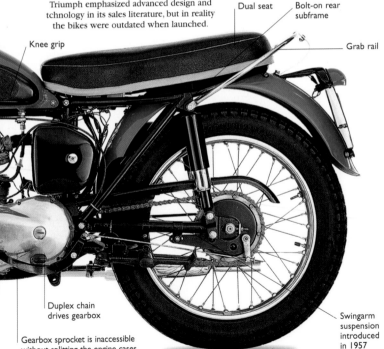

Dual seat

Bolt-on rear subframe

Grab rail

Knee grip

Duplex chain drives gearbox

Gearbox sprocket is inaccessible without splitting the engine cases

Swingarm suspension introduced in 1957

1959 T120 BONNEVILLE

• A TRADITIONAL TWIN WITH INCREASED POWER CAPACITY •

NAMED AFTER THE UTAH SALT FLATS on which a Triumph twin achieved a world speed record (see pp. 28–29), the T120 Bonneville was a high-performance version of Triumph's 650 twin introduced at the Earl's Court Show in 1958. Power was increased by fitting twin carburetors to an improved cylinder head (thus increasing the compression ratio) and using performance camshafts. The single downtube frame on this rare 1959 model was replaced by a duplex version in 1960.

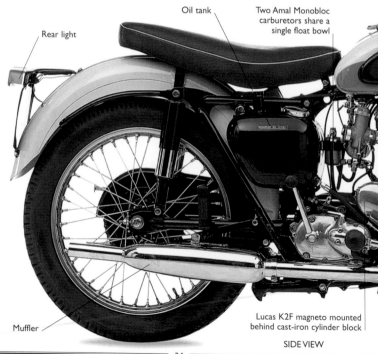

Oil tank

Two Amal Monobloc carburetors share a single float bowl

Rear light

Muffler

Lucas K2F magneto mounted behind cast-iron cylinder block

SIDE VIEW

SPECIFICATIONS

- **ENGINE** Overhead-valve, parallel twin
- **CAPACITY** 649cc
- **POWER OUTPUT** 46bhp @ 6,500rpm
- **TRANSMISSION** Four-speed
- **WEIGHT** 404lb (183kg)
- **TOP SPEED** 110mph (177km/h)

Speedometer

Last year of headlamp nacelle

Parcel rack

Fuel filler-cap

OVERHEAD VIEW

Two-tone paint job

"Mouth organ" tank badge

License plate

Single-frame downtube

Dynamo clamped across front of crankcase

1969 T150 TRIDENT

• TRIUMPH'S TRIPLE IS BORN •

DEMAND FOR MORE POWER LED motorcycle designers to build multi-cylinder machines. To avoid the costs of developing an all-new machine, Triumph effectively added another cylinder to its 500cc twin to create a 740cc triple. A 120° crankshaft made it smoother and better-sounding than the twin. The Trident was fast and handled well, but it couldn't compete with the glitzy and reliable four-cylinder Honda that appeared at the same time. It wasn't introduced into the UK until 1969, a year after its launch in export markets.

Passenger grab rail

Saddle release-knob

Three Amal Concentric carburetors

"Ray gun" muffler

Horn

Solidly mounted footrest

SIDE VIEW

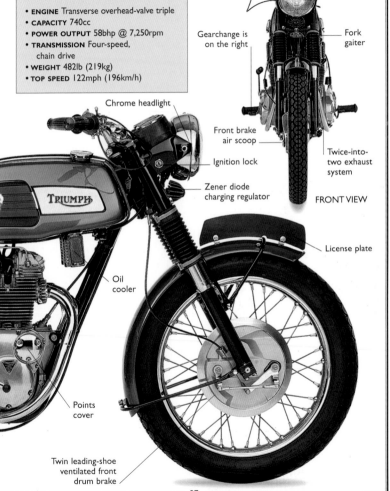

SPECIFICATIONS

- **ENGINE** Transverse overhead-valve triple
- **CAPACITY** 740cc
- **POWER OUTPUT** 58bhp @ 7,250rpm
- **TRANSMISSION** Four-speed, chain drive
- **WEIGHT** 482lb (219kg)
- **TOP SPEED** 122mph (196km/h)

Gearchange is on the right

Fork gaiter

Chrome headlight

Front brake air scoop

Ignition lock

Zener diode charging regulator

Twice-into-two exhaust system

FRONT VIEW

License plate

Oil cooler

TRIUMPH

Points cover

Twin leading-shoe ventilated front drum brake

1971 TRIDENT RACER

• KING OF TRIUMPH'S RACING BIKES •

TRIUMPH SHOWED LITTLE INTEREST in motorcycle racing until a production-based class became popular in Europe and America. In 1970 and '71, the factory race shop assembled special race bikes using tuned 750cc Trident engines fitted into lightweight racing frames. These fantastic machines outperformed and outhandled all opposition for two seasons, with big wins recorded on both sides of the Atlantic.

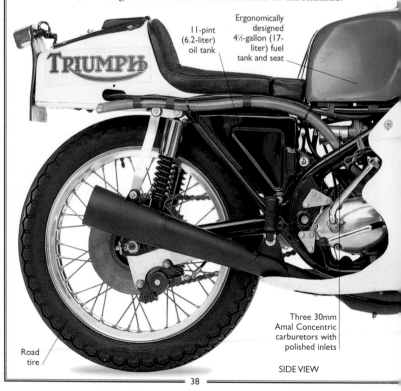

11-pint (6.2-liter) oil tank

Ergonomically designed 4½-gallon (17-liter) fuel tank and seat

Three 30mm Amal Concentric carburetors with polished inlets

Road tire

SIDE VIEW

Windshield

Fiberglass
fairing

Rev
counter

SPECIFICATIONS

- **ENGINE** In-line, air-cooled,
  three-cylinder
- **CAPACITY** 749cc
- **POWER OUTPUT** Over 70bhp
- **TRANSMISSION** Four-speed, chain drive
- **WEIGHT** 395lb (179kg)
- **TOP SPEED** 164mph (264km/h)

Angled headlight
gives maximum
visibility when
cornering

Lockheed
brake caliper

Twin cast-
iron drum
brakes

Light above race
number helps pit
crew record lap times

Three-into-one
exhaust system

Brake
pad

1979 T140D BONNEVILLE

• A CLASSIC LASTS FOR OVER 40 YEARS •

Based on a design dating from 1937, the Triumph Bonneville was, by the 1970s, well past its sell-by date. However, its charisma and handling kept it popular. By the end of the decade, capacity had grown to 750cc, and there were five speeds in the gearbox. The T140D model shown was built in 1979 and featured detail changes including cast wheels and the black and gold paint job. It may have looked good, but performance was poor – the engine was strangled by noise restrictions.

Passenger grab rail

Amal Mark 2 carburetors

Large rear light

Two-into-one exhaust system with restrictive muffler

Brake and gearchange operation switched sides in 1975 to comply with US legislation

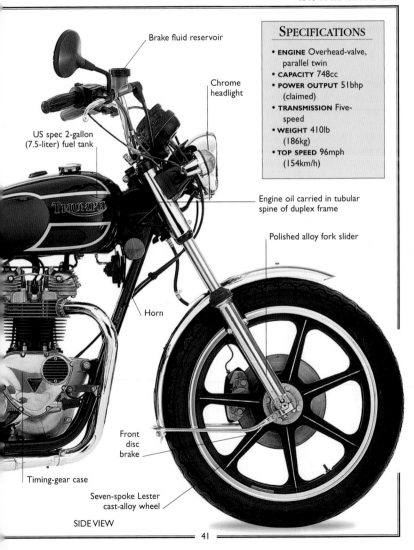

Brake fluid reservoir

Chrome headlight

US spec 2-gallon (7.5-liter) fuel tank

Engine oil carried in tubular spine of duplex frame

Polished alloy fork slider

Horn

Front disc brake

Timing-gear case

Seven-spoke Lester cast-alloy wheel

SIDE VIEW

SPECIFICATIONS

- **ENGINE** Overhead-valve, parallel twin
- **CAPACITY** 748cc
- **POWER OUTPUT** 51bhp (claimed)
- **TRANSMISSION** Five-speed
- **WEIGHT** 410lb (186kg)
- **TOP SPEED** 96mph (154km/h)

1997 T595 DAYTONA

• A STUNNING SUPERBIKE TO COMPETE WITH THE BEST •

SIX YEARS AFTER TRIUMPH'S 1991 relaunch, the company entered the lucrative supersports market with the T595, built to compete with the market-leading Honda Fireblade and charismatic Ducati 916. The bike used Triumph's trademark three-cylinder setup and the Daytona name from earlier models, but almost everything else was new. Though lighter, more powerful, and better-looking than its predecessor, the T595's reputation suffered when some early bikes had to be recalled due to a frame problem.

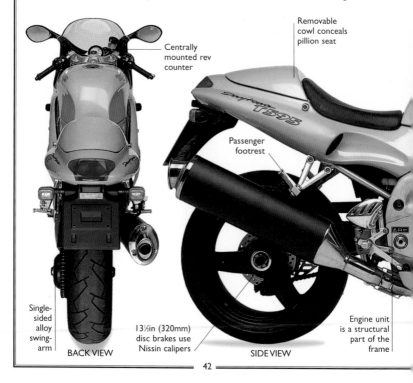

Centrally mounted rev counter

Removable cowl conceals pillion seat

Passenger footrest

Single-sided alloy swing-arm

13½in (320mm) disc brakes use Nissin calipers

Engine unit is a structural part of the frame

BACK VIEW

SIDE VIEW

SPECIFICATIONS

- **ENGINE** Twin camshaft, 12-valve, three-cylinder
- **CAPACITY** 955cc
- **POWER OUTPUT** 114bhp @ 9.500rpm
- **TRANSMISSION** Six-speed, chain drive
- **WEIGHT** 437lb (198kg)
- **TOP SPEED** 160mph (257km/h)

Front brake master cylinder

Clip-on handlebars

Aluminum perimeter frame incorporates an unusual tubular construction

Air intake

FRONT VIEW

2in (45mm) telescopic forks are adjustable for preload, compression, and rebound damping

Bridgestone BT56 tire

Quick-release fairing fastener

Radiator and air cooler hidden in fairing

Three-spoke alloy wheels made by Brembo of Italy

INDEX

ACKNOWLEDGMENTS

AUTHOR'S ACKNOWLEDGMENTS:
Thanks to Phil Hunt and Mark Johnson-Davies and to Louise Candlish, Tracy Hambleton-Miles, and everyone else at DK. Special thanks to Matty Ball for explaining the workings of the Triumph laughing shaft and giggling pin arrangement.

DORLING KINDERSLEY WOULD LIKE TO THANK THE FOLLOWING FOR THEIR ASSISTANCE:
Bikerama, London; Deutsches Zweirad Museum NSU Museum, Neckarsulm, Germany; Motorcycle Heritage Foundation, Westerville, Ohio; The National Motor Museum, Beaulieu, UK; and The National Motorcycle Museum, Birmingham, UK.

DORLING KINDERSLEY WOULD LIKE TO THANK THE FOLLOWING FOR THEIR KIND PERMISSION TO USE THEIR PHOTOGRAPHS:
Classic Bike/EMAP:
27 top center, 29 center, 31 bottom right.
Ricardo Consulting Engineers Ltd.:
21 top center.
All photography by Dave King and Andy Crawford.

NOTE
Every effort has been made to trace the copyright holders. Dorling Kindersley apologizes for any unintentional omissions and would be pleased, in such cases, to add an acknowledgment in future editions.